Original title:
The Happiness of Christmas Spirit

Copyright © 2024 Creative Arts Management OÜ
All rights reserved.

Author: Lucas Harrington
ISBN HARDBACK: 978-9916-90-974-4
ISBN PAPERBACK: 978-9916-90-975-1

Seasons of Love, Laughter, and Light

Spring brings joy, the flowers bloom,
In summer's heat, we bust a move.
Autumn's leaves dance down the lane,
While winter's chill makes us complain.

But through it all, laughter we find,
In goofy socks that 'don't' quite bind.
With every season, love's the prize,
It keeps us warm 'neath cloudy skies.

Soft Footsteps on a Snowy Path

The snowflakes fall, a soft white coat,
I slip and slide, oh what a goat!
I build a snowman, hat askew,
He looks more sad than jolly too.

My toes are numb, I lose my way,
In search of cocoa on this day.
Each step I take, a wobbly dance,
I'm half a clown in winter's trance.

The Taste of Familiar Delights

Grandma's cookies, oh what a treat,
They stick to my gums, quite the feat.
Her secret's magic, so she claims,
But we all know it's butter games.

Pizza Fridays, cheese galore,
I eat too much, then ask for more.
Each bite a hug, a friend in cheese,
With every slice, my heart's at ease.

A Mosaic of Festive Greetings

Christmas lights flicker, what a sight,
I trip on cords—oh what a fright!
The cards come pouring, some are late,
Uncle Bob's jokes- they just can't wait.

New Year's Eve with hats askew,
Champagne spills, and laughter too.
With resolutions made in cheer,
Let's raise a glass to another year!

Heartstrings Pulled with Joy

When life gives you lemons, make a pie,
But don't forget to blink, or you'll cry.
Dance like a potato, find your groove,
A silly jig is how we move.

Socks on your hands, the new fashion craze,
Unicycle riding through the sun's rays.
Balloons in the sky, float up with glee,
Life's a circus, come laugh with me.

Sleds and Smiles Against the Snow

Sledding down the hill, a glorious ride,
Face full of snow, oh what a slide!
We tumble and roll, a snowball fight,
With laughter and shrieks, pure delight.

Hot cocoa waiting, marshmallows galore,
Warming our toes by the crackling floor.
A snowman is grinning, can't stop his style,
With a carrot nose, he's been here a while.

Serene Moments, Lively Hearts

In the garden, the gnomes dance around,
Chasing the butterflies, never a frown.
The breeze whispers secrets to the trees,
While squirrels hold meetings over berries and cheese.

A hammock swings gently, inviting a nap,
But a kitten around, it's a joyful trap.
She pounces with glee, fluffs the soft air,
Serene moments explode with laughter and flair.

Wreaths of Gratitude and Joy

Wreaths on the door, all bows and cheer,
Kittens are hiding, come peek, oh dear!
With carols sung out in the midst of the fun,
Ho ho ho, here comes the pun!

Gather 'round friends, let's eat all the pie,
Our hearts are so full, we just might fly.
A toast to our laughter, together we say,
Life's a feast of love, each and every day.

Sweet Serenity in the Chill

Snowflakes dance, they swirl and spin,
While I'm bundled up, cozy within.
The cat's plotting mischief, I see him lurk,
As I sip my cocoa, that fluffy jerk.

Frosty windows, drawing shapes with my breath,
This winter's chill sure beats my ex's wrath.
The fireplace crackles, what a lovely sound,
A warm, comfy blanket is perfectly found.

Gentle Murmurs of A Winter's Eve

Underneath stars, so bright and bold,
I tripped on a snowbank, just like I'm told.
My dog's got a sweater, it's quite the sight,
He struts like a model, what a delight!

Hot soup on the stove, oh what a show,
As I watch my neighbor slip, landing face-first in snow.
With every little giggle, the chilly winds blow,
At least I'll have stories in case I'm too slow.

A Hearth Warming with Light

Logs on the fire, they pop and they crack,
As I debate snacks – should I have a whole pack?
The smell of baked cookies floats through the air,
Though with all my baking, there's none to share.

The cats curl up tight, they've claimed both my knees,
While I'm lost in a blanket, searching for cheese.
A movie's starting, but I can't quite see,
Between the snacks and the cats, it's just me!

Mirthful Echoes in Starry Nights

Stars twinkle bright, but I can't find a way,
To dodge the coffee stains from my coffee today.
As I gaze at the sky, with a grin on my face,
I remember that I forgot my purse in that place!

With laughter shared under the moon's soft glow,
We recall the time I tried to make snow glow.
But hey, what's the harm? We'll laugh till we cry,
As the universe chuckles, and so do I!

The Delight of Timeless Rituals

Morning coffee spills, oh what a sight,
The cat's in the cup, giving me fright.
My toast plays music, it's all burnt jazz,
Breakfast ballet, what an awkward pizzazz.

Socks in the dryer, a dance of their own,
They tumble and twist, like seeds that are blown.
I count them, I sigh, where do they all go?
My lonely left sock, he's a part of the show.

Dishwashers sing with a clink and a clatter,
While puddles of spaghetti cause all sorts of chatter.
My fork joins a symphony under the foam,
Oh, the delight of rituals that feel like home!

In the evening, my slippers perform a sweet waltz,
They shuffle in rhythm, never have faults.
As I collapse on the couch, they cheer and they squeak,
Life's timeless rituals, quirky and unique!

Whimsical Dreams in the Frosty Night

Under a blanket of sparkly white,
The snowman wears shades, quite a funny sight.
He greets me with waves, a frosty 'hello!',
His carrot nose winks, like a star in the glow.

Penguins in bow ties, sliding with glee,
They twirl on the ice, oh how wild and free!
A snowball fight starts with laughter and cheer,
But I duck behind trees, my fate's looking clear.

I dream of a unicorn sipping hot tea,
Telling me secrets of magical glee.
The teapot's a dragon, all fiery and grand,
Whimsical tales from a frosty wonderland!

With cocoa and marshmallows, cozy I lie,
As snowflakes like fairies dance down from the sky.
In whimsical dreams, all silly and bright,
The frosty night sparkles with pure delight!

Boughs Bursting with Goodwill

Boughs of the tree hang low with delight,
Each ornament tells tales of merry night.
A squirrel wears tinsel, a star on its head,
Finding nutty treasures under the spread.

The lights start to twinkle, a bumpy parade,
As garlands of popcorn begin to cascade.
The dog gets a tinsel crown, oh what a sight,
He prances like royalty, full of delight!

Pinecones are singing their spiky ol' song,
'Join in the fun, it won't be long!'
They tumble together, a merry old show,
Boughs bursting with goodwill, oh what a glow!

Under the moonlight, the moment is bright,
The laughter of friends turns shadows to light.
With cocoa in hand, the joy starts to spill,
Boughs bursting with goodwill, our hearts they fulfill!

Candied Melodies in Twilight's Glow

In the kitchen, a symphony's brewing tonight,
Cookies are dancing, oh what a sight!
Brownies are crooning a gooey old song,
I hum along softly; it won't take long.

Candy canes whistle and marshmallows sway,
As gingerbread men begin to ballet.
Sprinkles are flying, a sugary storm,
Candied melodies, keeping us warm.

The pie starts to giggle, it's crusty but sweet,
Laughter erupts with each buttery beat.
The spatula leads a charmed, wild dance,
Under the glow, we all take a chance.

So gather around as we share every bite,
With joy in our hearts and flavors so bright.
Twilight's alive with sweet jingles that show,
Candied melodies in the warm golden glow!

Cherished Stories by Candlelight

In the glow of candle's light,
We tell tales of silly fright.
A cat that danced upon a hat,
And chased a mouse that looked like that!

Grandpa's stories take their time,
About a cow that learned to rhyme.
With every word, we laugh and tease,
As shadows flicker in the breeze.

A knight who had a fear of heights,
Would fly by plane to win the fights.
The dragon snorted soup instead,
With noodles tangled 'round its head.

So here's a toast to memoirs bright,
Where every tale brings pure delight.
Together we'll create more lore,
By candlelight, forevermore!

Harmonies of Hope and Joy

In a world where socks go missing,
We find the tunes that keep us kissing.
A symphony of giggles bright,
Echoing through the day and night.

A bird that sings with a lisp so sweet,
Calls out to folks with rhythmic feet.
Dancing in laughter under a tree,
Let's harmonize, just you and me!

While we bake a cake that flops,
We hum a tune and do the hops.
Five eggs cracked and shells all around,
But the laughter's the best sound!

So grab your friends, let's sing a long,
In this chorus, we'll never go wrong.
With hope and joy, we'll fill our cups,
And let the beat of laughter erupt!

A Chorus of Laughter and Delight

When chickens try to cross the road,
You'll find a tale that's often told.
With each small step, the giggles grow,
As they dodge cars moving slow.

Then there's the cat who chased its tail,
In circles round without fail.
It tripped and flipped into a pot,
Now dinner's served – it's quite a lot!

With silly jokes that make us yell,
About a fish who learned to spell.
His words got tangled every time,
But we still laugh, oh isn't it prime?

So let's sing out in chorus clear,
With every chuckle, more good cheer.
In laughter's glow, we find our way,
Delighting hearts along the way!

Lights that Sparkle with Kindness

Under stars that twinkle bright,
We share our dreams with pure delight.
A light bulb that just won't behave,
Sparks laughter when it starts to wave.

A puppy dressed in glitter gear,
Chases a cat while we all cheer.
With kindness wrapped in bows and ties,
Their friendship blooms, oh what a prize!

In every smile, a shine so true,
Like fireflies in the evening dew.
They light the way with hugs and cheer,
Spreading love, bringing hearts near.

So let's be lights in darkened skies,
With kindness shining through our eyes.
Together we'll sparkle, understand,
Creating a world that's truly grand!

Stars that Dance on Frosted Whispers

Under the moon, they twist and twirl,
Snowflakes thinking they can whirl.
Stars giggle as they shine so bright,
While frost claims victory for the night.

Penguins waddle, trying to prance,
In their tuxedos, they take a chance.
A comet trips on a chilly breeze,
And all the cosmos bursts into wheezes.

An astronaut joins the frostball fun,
Tossing snowballs, oh what a run!
The Milky Way drops a frosty glance,
Eggnog flows—now let's all dance!

With every flake that drifts and sways,
Laughter echoes in snowy displays.
So let us frolic beneath this trance,
As stars keep dancing—what a chance!

Warmth Wrapped in Red and Green

A cozy blanket, red and green,
Hot cocoa spills—oh, what a scene!
Marshmallows fluff in frothy whips,
But somehow end up in nose-tipped sips!

The Christmas tree, a glorious sight,
Ornaments clashing in wild delight.
A cat takes aim after the garland,
And suddenly it's like a warland!

Gingerbread men with spicy charm,
One bites back—it's quite the alarm!
Sprinkled sugar, icing galore,
But one sweet dude ran out the door!

Ribbons tangled in a festive knot,
Everyone's laughing, forget-me-not!
In this chaos, joy truly leans,
Wrapped in laughter, red and greens.

Memories Made in Scented Pines

Oh, the forest smells like cozy dreams,
Under tall pines with whispering schemes.
Children giggle, hiding behind trees,
While squirrels comment with tiny wheezes.

Cookies burnt; the kitchen's a mess,
Mom's recipe isn't—oh, what stress!
A sprinkle of chaos, a pinch of cheer,
And nighttime tales bring everyone near.

The fire crackles, warmth all around,
With marshmallows roasting—sweet gooey sound.
Dad tells stories of times gone past,
While laughter and memories pour out fast.

In the scent of pines, together we leap,
Making memories we'll treasure and keep.
Through laughter and joy, our hearts entwine,
Forever remembered, in fragrant pines.

Laughter Lingers in the Air

As snowflakes dance and giggles bloom,
Pies and cookies invade the room.
A dog in a hat is chasing its tail,
While grandpa's stories seem to regale.

Kids trade jokes, oh what a sight,
One tells a pun, sends the cat in fright!
Uncle's wig slips, with a comical flair,
And laughter lingers in the cold air.

A snowman dons a stick as a pipe,
With a carrot nose, he's quite the type.
A snowball fight breaks into glee,
As laughter rings out—what a jubilee!

So gather 'round for a winter's cheer,
With giggles and grins to last all year.
In this joyous season, hearts are laid bare,
Where laughter lingers in the cool air.

Cradled in Warm Memories

In a box labeled 'Memories',
I found my old report cards,
Each grade a surprise, you see,
Like finding candy in shards.

Grandma's cookies, burnt to crisp,
We laughed, she swore they were great,
We each tried not to gulp and gasp,
As we chewed, sealed our fate.

Old photos with wild hairstyles,
Our fashion sense, quite a joke,
We grinned through all of our trials,
So cool, we were just a hoax.

Now I sit with coffee hot,
Reflecting on all the quirks,
These memories, they really knot,
Our laughter, where friendship lurks.

Radiance of Familiar Faces

At the coffee shop, they greet,
With names as weird as a treat,
With a smile so wide, like the sun,
It's unfiltered joy, pure fun.

Bob, with jokes that fall like lead,
Yet every laugh is golden thread,
Sally's tales go on and on,
Like soap operas at the dawn.

They say I wear my coffee well,
Just like a badge, an art to sell,
With cream on my nose, they know,
I'm thriving in this morning glow.

Each face is familiar, a song,
Where I feel that I truly belong,
These moments, oh, so divine,
Each smiling face a bright sign.

Embers of Warmth in the Chill

Winter nights bring frosty air,
But inside, we've got a flare,
Hot cocoa tops with a marshmallow,
Melting dreams, like soft, sweet pillows.

Blankets wrapped, we snugly hide,
Though outside howling winds collide,
Here, the laughter's warm and wide,
Like snuggling a thousand pies.

Evenings spent with silly games,
Chasing points, not seeking fame,
With every quirky move we make,
We're warming hearts, make no mistake.

So let the cold winds blow and twirl,
Inside, we've got a cozy whirl,
With spirit bright, we fill the chill,
And laugh our way through winter's thrill.

A Quilt of Joyful Connections

Friendship stitched with threads of cheer,
Woven tight, we hold each dear,
Each laugh a patch, each tear a seam,
Creating warmth as we live the dream.

Gathered round the table spread,
Silly stories joyously said,
We feast on love, pie in hand,
Delicious bonds we have so planned.

Shared secrets and goofy eyes,
Crafting memories, oh what a prize,
Every hug like a quilted square,
Wrapped in care, everywhere we share.

A tapestry of heart and glee,
In this quilt, we're truly free,
Connected tightly, stitched for good,
Our laughter echoes, as it should.

Joyful Hearts Gather Around

Joyful hearts gather around,
With laughter and cheer, it's profound.
We're sharing our snacks, oh so divine,
And stealing your fries? That's just fine!

The snowflakes dance, a waltz in the air,
But Aunt Martha's sweater is quite a scare.
We toast with cocoa, cheers all around,
Who knew such joy could be so profound?

Uncle Joe's jokes, they never get old,
Like stories of treasures and legends retold.
We're wrapped in warmth, like a burrito,
With puns and giggles, watch me go!

As the night deepens, our spirits soar,
With playful bickering, who can ask for more?
Joyful hearts gather, hand in hand,
Dancing in circles, it's all so grand!

The Gift of Togetherness

The gift of togetherness, wrapped up tight,
With bows of laughter that shine so bright.
We swap silly stories, and socks with holes,
In this sharing season, we barter our souls.

Grandma's fudge is a sticky delight,
A sugary challenge that fights with your bite.
We gather 'round tables, feast like kings,
While discussing the merits of fruitcake flings!

In the chaos of wrapping, we giggle and fight,
For the last roll of tape most ridiculous sight.
But deep down we know, despite all the fuss,
It's together we cherish, in love and in trust.

So here's to our quirks and our holiday cheer,
To the hugs that we share, and the stuff we hold dear.
The gift of togetherness, priceless and bold,
Is the laughter we share, a treasure to hold!

Serenade of Cheerful Carols

We sing a serenade of cheerful carols,
Off-key and loud, like musical ferals.
The cat's on the roof, in absolute shock,
While we belt out tunes, each one a block!

With sleigh bells ringing, we're on a roll,
Forgotten the lyrics, it takes its toll.
But who cares about notes when spirit's so high?
Just give us some chocolate, and we'll surely fly!

The neighbors are peeking, confused as can be,
While we dance in our socks, it's a sight to see.
With joy in our hearts and a giggle or two,
This caroling crew is the best of the crew!

So jingle those bells and let laughter resound,
In this jolly season, let friendship be found.
A serenade fills the frosty night air,
With each silly note, we are free without care!

Soft Hues of Holiday Bliss

In soft hues of holiday bliss,
The world turns magical, can't give it a miss.
With lights that twinkle like stars in the night,
We sip on our cocoa, everything's right!

The cookies are burning, what a tragic fate,
But who needs to bake? We've got a great plate!
With laughter and love in grand supply,
Let's eat those burnt cookies, oh me, oh my!

Snowmen are built, with a carrot for flair,
But they melt down quick, with warmth in the air.
As we gather 'round, with stories to tell,
Our hearts are aglow, under this holiday spell.

With memories made, as bright as the lights,
We cherish these moments, the smiles and delights.
In soft hues of holiday bliss, we embrace,
Each giggle, each hug, and a warm, happy face!

Snowflakes and Smiles in Harmonious Dance

Snowflakes whisper softly, oh so light,
They twirl around, a frosty delight.
Children giggle, bundled in gear,
While snowmen smile from ear to ear.

Snowball fights erupt in all their glory,
With laughter shared, they write their story.
Hot cocoa waits, a steamy embrace,
As cheeks turn rosy, a joyful race.

Magic fills the air, in swirling white,
Each flake's a dancer, pure delight.
Snowflakes and smiles, hand in hand,
Together they frolic, across the land.

Fireside Tales and Cocoa Dreams

Crackling fires and shadows play,
Tales of dragons waltz away.
With marshmallows toasted to a nice brown,
Giggles erupt and no one wears a frown.

Sipping cocoa with extra cheers,
We laugh aloud, erasing fears.
Stories twist with a silly spin,
Imaginations wake, let the fun begin!

Grandpa's yarns filled with quirky sights,
Of talking cats and paper kites.
Fireside magic that warms the soul,
In this tapestry, we're perfectly whole.

Enchanted Nights Full of Laughter

Stars are twinkling, a shady glow,
Under blankets, we all huddle low.
Whispers of humor weave through the air,
As we share silly stories, joys to share.

A glowing moon, a glowing grin,
With laughter echoing, we let it begin.
Tickling toes and playful jests,
Making spirit soar, we give it our best.

Knock-knock jokes fly like night birds,
Filling the dark with laughter's words.
Enchanting nights where mirth survives,
In every chuckle, pure joy thrives.

A Tapestry of Joyful Gatherings

Gather 'round the table, so divine,
With food and friends, the stars align.
Stories unfold, rich and bright,
Belly laughs explode through the night.

Games and snacks, oh what a mix!
Playing charades with all the tricks.
A chorus of giggles, a whimsical song,
In this patchwork of joy, we all belong.

Grandma's pie sings a sugary tune,
As we share our dreams beneath the moon.
Tapestries woven with laughter's art,
Gatherings cherished, straight from the heart.

Glimpse of Hope Amidst the Frost

In winter's chill, I found a sock,
It's missing its mate, still, I can't mock,
A glimmer of hope in the frosty air,
Just one odd sock, well, life's not fair.

The snowflakes dance with a merry cheer,
But my frozen toes just want a beer,
The cocoa's warm, but where's the marshmallows?
Oh look, a squirrel! He's stealing my pillows.

Ice on the pond, where the ducks plop down,
They waddle and slip, in a snowy gown,
I chuckle and watch as they put on a show,
A splash and a honk, my heart's all aglow.

So here's to the frost, that tickles our nose,
A glimpse of hope, in all this cold prose,
Life's little joys in the snowflakes bright,
Makes winter a canvas of whimsical light.

The Joyful Glow of Familiar Faces

Gather around, the crew's in town,
With laughter and stories, we'll wear the crown,
A pot of hot stew and bread fresh-baked,
Joyful glow, like a family, well-staked.

A slip on the ice, who cares? Just fall,
We'll laugh 'til we cry, and that's not all,
With each hearty joke, we bridge the space,
The warmth of our voices, a sweet embrace.

Old photos flash, with hairstyles so bold,
The fashion disaster turns to pure gold,
In every smile, our memories grow,
Familiar faces, the best show in tow.

So raise a glass to these moments dear,
With every laugh, we hold them near,
In winter's grasp, we light up the way,
With joyful glow, we'll forever stay.

Winter's Breath, Soft and Warm

Winter's breath whispers, soft and clear,
It tickles our cheeks, brings forth a cheer,
Hot chocolate's calling, marshmallows afloat,
As snowflakes dance, like a playful goat.

We bundle up tight, in jackets so bright,
Looking like marshmallows, what a sight!
To sled down the hill, we scream and we glide,
With mittens and laughter, joy as our guide.

The silence of night, as snow blankets low,
Footprints of critters, where did they go?
The warmth of a fire adds spice to the chill,
With tales that bring giggles, and windows that thrill.

So here's to the season of frost and delight,
Where comfort and warmth outshine the night,
In winter's embrace, we find our way home,
With memories forged, together we roam.

A Reverie of Shared Joys

In the kitchen we dance, what a sight,
With flour on faces, oh what delight.
A cupcake erupts, frosting's on the wall,
Our laughter rings out, a sweet-hearted call.

We trip on our socks, like clumsy old bears,
In a battle of tickles, no one really cares.
The cat, she just watches, with judgmental eyes,
As we roll on the floor, in delightful surprise.

A movie that's silent, yet laughter's too loud,
With popcorn explosions, a slapstick crowd.
We fall off the couch, in a fit of pure glee,
In this reverie shared, it's just you and me.

So here's to these moments, we treasure so dear,
With giggles and snorts, and a sprinkle of cheer.
Together we whirl through this silly parade,
In joy's grand creation, our memories are made.

Laughter Echoing in the Cold

Wrapped up like burritos, we step out into frost,
Slipping on ice, all our footing is lost.
We gather our courage, give it one more try,
Then boom! Down goes Tim, like a potato in pie.

Snowflakes are falling, each one with a jest,
A snowball flung fiercely, he's anyone's guest.
The wind whistles tunes that are silly and bold,
As laughter rings out, in the shimmering cold.

With noses all red, and toes feeling numb,
We build a great snowman, his name is "Dum-Dum."
We chat about life as we sculpt with finesse,
Each giggle's an echo, a warm, cozy mess.

When the evening sets in, hot cocoa's a must,
With marshmallows diving, it's a chocolaty crust.
Through laughter and snow, our spirits take flight,
In this chilly embrace, our hearts feel so light.

Wishes Carried on the Wind

On the hilltop we sat, with our wishes in hand,
A balloon full of giggles, we released on demand.
It floated away, like our hopes in the breeze,
With dreams full of laughter, we felt so at ease.

We tossed out our fears, like confetti in air,
As butterflies danced, losing worries, we dare.
Our wishes took flight, on a comical quest,
For more joy to gather, in this life we're blessed.

The wind howled a tune, of childhood delight,
Turning our whispers into a whimsical flight.
A song of our laughter, like bubbles, they burst,
With each joyful chime, our excitement rehearsed.

So here's to the wishes we send on the wind,
To the laughter and fun, as true friends we've pinned.
In this playful embrace, let the giggles unbind,
For wishes and laughter are two of a kind.

A Tidal Wave of Joyous Memories

At the beach with our buckets, we set out to play,
Digging up treasures in the hot sandy sway.
But a wave had a secret, it leapt for a splash,
And drenched all our hopes in a watery crash.

We tumbled and giggled, in the sea's wide embrace,
Like fish out of water, we floundered in grace.
With seagulls proclaiming our goofy, loud cheer,
While sand mixed with laughter, that echoed so clear.

The sunshine was bright, but our spirits shined more,
As we danced on the shore, letting happiness soar.
Each grain holds a story, as we build castles tall,
In this tidal wave of joy, let's remember it all.

So here's to our moments, the bright and the strange,
To the laughter and mishaps, our perfect exchange.
We'll carry this treasure, wherever we roam,
In the tidal wave of memories, we've found our true home.

Beneath the Mistletoe's Gentle Spell

In December's chill we gather,
With twinkling lights and laughter,
A kiss beneath the mistletoe,
Then blame it on the afterglow.

Uncle Joe starts to prance,
His dancing skills? Not by chance!
He bumps into the Christmas tree,
Now it's a festive sight to see!

Cookies crumbling in our hands,
Watch out for the cookie bands!
Rats in Santa hats, they roam,
Scavenging our Christmas home!

So raise a glass, let's toast tonight,
To relatives, who add delight;
We'll laugh and cheer, forget the stress,
Beneath the mistletoe's sweet mess!

A Time for Giving, a Time for Joy

Underneath the Christmas tree,
Presents stacked—oh, woe is me!
I gave away my last clean shirt,
In hopes of not eating dessert!

Grandma's knitting—what a sight,
A scarf that's three feet wide and tight,
It looks like a colorful beast,
Merry Christmas—now I'm released!

Ribbons tangled, chaos swirls,
Kids are screaming, hearts in twirls,
Yet, in all this joyful noise,
We find our love, our truest joys!

So when the gifts are all unwrapped,
And tummy troubles have been trapped,
It's love we share—it's here to stay,
A time for giving, hip-hip-hooray!

Hearts Kindled by the Spirit of Giving.

With warm cocoa in hand we sit,
Binge-watching one more holiday skit,
"The office party" is the best—
I'm all in for the chocolate quest!

Neighbors come with pie in tow,
But no one knows just who made dough;
They argue who's the pumpkin king,
As jingle bells and laughter ring!

Kids dressed like little reindeer,
Prancing round without any fear,
They stomp and crash, a total mess,
While we pretend it's all finesse!

Hearts aglow with laughter bright,
In this wacky, silly night;
Through all the festive giggles and grins,
We kindle love where fun begins!

Joyful Whispers of Winter

Winter whispers, soft and sweet,
With snowflakes dancing at our feet,
I slipped on ice, oh what a sight,
My dignity took quite a flight!

Sledding down the hill, oh please,
We scream and shout—no time for freeze!
But wait, who's that all dressed in red?
Just a cat who thinks he's sled!

The carolers sing off-key at best,
Yet we applaud—a merry jest!
With jingle bells in hand we sway,
And hope they don't sing all day!

So let's embrace the winter cheer,
With laughter and a cozy beer;
For joy comes not just from the snow,
But from the love we gladly show!

Enchanted Moments by the Fire

In the glow of flames we sit,
Telling tales that make us split.
S'mores are burnt, but who will care?
We laugh and sing, with messy hair.

The marshmallows fly like shooting stars,
One hit my dad right on the bars!
He jumped and twirled in surprise,
As laughter echoed 'neath night skies.

The shadows dance upon the ground,
With every shadow, joy is found.
The crackling fire keeps us warm,
While silly stories take their form.

With friends around and hearts so light,
We'll share this magic every night.
So if you hear a ghostly cheer,
Just know it's fun—grab another beer!

A Tapestry of Smiles and Wishes

A quilt of laughter on the floor,
Where giggles and wishes we store.
Each stitch a tale of silly grace,
With happy faces in every space.

We weave our dreams with vibrant threads,
Like wildflowers sprouting from our heads.
A tapestry made of marshmallow fluff,
With pockets of joy and just enough.

Each corner holds a silly joke,
Like 'Why did the chicken cross the yoke?'
To dance under the disco lights,
And make the toasters join the fights!

So gather 'round, let stories flow,
With smiles as bright as the moon's glow.
We'll stitch together, hand in hand,
A tapestry, both wild and grand!

Glowing Memories Beneath the Tree

Beneath the branches, laughter rings,
Like bells announcing joyful things.
We hide from cats, who stalk with flair,
Pretending to be gifts dressed with care.

The twinkling lights upon the tree,
From tangled mess, they set us free.
As tinsel falls and sparkles shine,
We dance around like it's divine.

Each ornament tells a whacky tale,
Of cousin Bob who turned quite pale,
When he found the bugs inside his cake,
We laughed so hard—our sides did ache!

Hot cocoa spills on grandma's shoes,
But oh, what fun to share our blues.
With glowing memories, we are a team,
Beneath the tree, we live our dream!

Wrapped in Love's Embrace

In cozy blankets, we all snuggle tight,
With popcorn flying in our delight.
The movie starts, but we're the show,
As jokes and giggles start to flow.

With faces scrunched in silly poses,
Like porcupines disguised as roses.
We share our snacks, both big and small,
While dodging crumbs that hit the wall.

A pillow fight breaks out, oh no!
And suddenly the cat's in the flow.
It's a wild ride of fluffy joy,
With squeaks and bounces, oh boy, oh boy!

So here's to hugs and goofy grins,
To all the love that always wins.
Wrapped in laughter, we find our place,
In this funny, warm embrace!

Echoes of Mirthful Nights

The moon's a giant disco ball,
With dance moves made of cheese,
We twirl around and nearly fall,
As laughter floats on breezy leaves.

The socks we wore, mismatched and bright,
Told stories of our wild delight,
A dance-off that went on till dawn,
With neighbors peeking, yawning, drawn.

We donned our hats like creatures rare,
Princess crowns paired with teddy bears,
In our parade, we pranced with glee,
Echoes of mirth, just you and me.

So here's to nights we won't forget,
With giggles as our safety net,
In every chuckle, every cheer,
Our hearts unite, forever near.

Frosted Laughter in the Air

On snowy days, we slip and slide,
Like penguins on a frosty glide,
Snowballs fly with joyful shouts,
While laughter echoes, no doubts.

The carrots for our snowmen's noses,
Got eaten by dogs, their frosty poses,
With frosted whiskers, they all stared,
Our snowman dreams, now quite impaired.

Hot cocoa spills on extra thick,
From mugs that leave a chocolaty slick,
We giggle still, despite the mess,
Frosted laughter, our happiness.

So raise a cup to winter's cheer,
With friends around, we have no fear,
Let snowflakes dance, let giggles fly,
In frosted joy, we reach the sky.

A Glimmer of Yuletide Cheer

The tree is up, the lights ablaze,
With tinsel tangled in a maze,
We search for ornaments, oh what fun,
But end up wearing bells—we've won!

We bake the cookies, dough on our nose,
The cat steals one, and off he goes,
In a blur of paws and fluffy fur,
A merry chase, a laughing stir!

The carols sung, we sing off-key,
But that gives us a chance to spree,
With every note, our hearts do soar,
In holiday joy, we ask for more.

So here's to cheer, bright and loud,
In every moment, let laughter shroud,
A glimmer shines on this festive night,
With love and joy, all spirits bright.

Radiant Hearts in Cozy Corners

In cozy corners, we convene,
With fairy lights, a soft sheen,
The cookies warm, they steal the show,
As we recount our tales with glow.

The cats are napping, dreams in fur,
While we reminisce, with every purr,
Each joke we crack ignites a spark,
Radiant hearts light up the dark.

Grandpa's stories, wild and sweet,
Of dancing bears and silly feats,
We laugh until the night is late,
In cozy corners, we celebrate.

So raise your glass, let laughter ring,
For every joy that moments bring,
In these warm hearts, we will remain,
Together, through sunshine and rain.

Joyful Echoes of Winter Nights

Snowflakes dancing in the air,
Hot cocoa spills, but who would care?
Sipping slowly, feeling bright,
Laughing loud through the cold night.

Frosty faces, cheeks so red,
Slip and slide, fall on your head!
Snowmen grinning, carrot nose,
Winter tales that nobody knows.

Sledding down the hill so steep,
All the promises that we keep.
Bundled tight, we chase the light,
Joyful echoes fill the night.

Carolers singing, voices clear,
Presents waiting, full of cheer.
Each cold breath, a puff of air,
Winter magic, everywhere!

Twinkling Lights and Warm Embraces

Twinkling lights on every tree,
Trying to reach them, can't you see?
Stumbling over tangled wires,
Laughter comes, igniting fires.

Warm embraces in the chill,
Hot meals served, with extra spill.
Friends all gather, stories shared,
Memories made, nobody spared.

Grandma's cookies, extra sweet,
All the joy is quite the treat.
Fires crackling, shadows play,
With every smile, we light the way.

Champagne bubbles, laughter loud,
Dancing like we're in a crowd.
With every hug, the world's alright,
In cozy rooms on winter nights!

Whispers of Mirth Beneath the Tree

Under the tree, presents piled high,
Sneaky peeks, oh, don't be shy!
Whispers echo, secrets shared,
Anticipation showed we cared.

Cats knock down the shimmering balls,
Dog's convinced the whole tree falls.
Tinsel tangled in your hair,
Endless giggles fill the air.

Gift wrapping skills are put to test,
Did I mention my dress is a mess?
Ribbons untie, chaos begins,
Laughter wins, nobody sins.

A season's spark in every glance,
Let's all join this merry dance.
Mirth beneath the tree so bright,
Making memories feels so right!

A Season's Gift of Love and Laughter

Mistletoe hung, cheeky grin,
A kiss requested, let's begin.
Awkward moments, shy and sweet,
Laughter erupts, can't be beat.

Gift exchanges that go awry,
"Oh this sweater, why oh why?"
Homemade treats, with a bite,
Gingerbread men in a food fight.

Slippers squeaking on the floor,
The dog escapes, and runs out the door.
Family feuds over board games,
Yet, somehow, love still remains.

So raise a glass, toast up high,
A season's gift, here's the why:
Love and laughter, we hold dear,
In every heart, it's always near!

Tinsel Dreams and Sugarplum Delights

Tinsel hanging from the trees,
Cats think it's their favorite tease.
Sugarplums bounce around with glee,
While grandpa snoozes with a sneeze.

Frosty windows, cold as ice,
Children pouting, thinking twice.
"Why is it so darn chilly here?"
Mom just shows them hot cocoa cheer!

Elves are busy stealing treats,
While reindeer munch on leftover beets.
Santa's stuck in the chimney tight,
"Next year, I'll order a smaller bite!"

Jingle bells and laughter loud,
Little ones make mom so proud.
A holiday filled with joy and mirth,
Who knew chaos could bring such worth?

Warmth Beneath the Starry Sky

Warmed by love beneath the night,
Kids are dreaming of pure delight.
Snowmen are dancing to songs so jolly,
While the dog chases glittery folly.

Socks are mismatched, what a sight!
Sipping cocoa feels just right.
Dad forgets the carol words,
But belts them out with joyful birds.

Stars are winking down at us,
As puppies join the festive fuss.
Hot chocolate spills, no need to frown,
A warm embrace makes winter a crown.

Fuzzy blankets piled up high,
Tickling toes that catch the eye.
For every giggle, there's a smile,
In the warmth, we'll stay awhile!

Candles Flickering with Hope

Candles flicker in the gloom,
Lights that chase away the doom.
Mom's cooking up her famous pies,
While the kids cover up their eyes.

Uncle Joe starts to tell a tale,
About the time he met a whale.
Or was it a fish? Or maybe a frog?
Either way, it left the family in a smog!

Tie up the dog, don't let him roam,
He's after leftovers, far from home.
Candles drip, making quite the mess,
Just like grandpa in his holiday dress!

Hopes are high, all feeling blessed,
A night of laughter, that's the best.
With flickering candles lighting the room,
We'll sing and dance away the gloom!

Snowflakes Dance to a Festive Tune

Snowflakes twirl in the cool night air,
Dancing like they just don't care.
Kids bundled up, laughing with glee,
Until they tumble, just wait and see!

Sleds are zooming down the track,
"Try not to fall!" echoes back.
Snowball fights start up with a shout,
Then someone cries, "Let's all go out!"

Frosty noses, rosy cheeks,
Who knew winter had such peaks?
Snowmen with silly hats and sticks,
They all join in on the winter tricks!

As the night deepens, hot cocoa calls,
We gather 'round, and laughter falls.
Snowflakes swirl, the night feels right,
Dancing till we say goodnight!

Twinkling Lights of Delight

The lights twinkle bright, oh what a sight,
They flicker and dance, bringing pure delight.
A cat's on the tree, what a daring feat,
I hope he won't munch on those cookies I heat.

With popcorn in hand, we laugh till we cry,
A snowman outside gives a wink as he sighs.
The dog steals a gift and runs off in glee,
Oh, what a night, come join in, and see!

The stockings are hung, but we see with dread,
That one's a bit ripped; it could spoil our spread.
Yet laughter erupts as we make merry cheer,
Singing loud tunes until the dawn's near.

So here's to the mischief and all that it brings,
The joy of this season, it makes our hearts sing.
In twinkling lights, we find our own way,
We chuckle and grin, let's celebrate today!

Cherished Moments in Whimsical Nights

Underneath the moonlight, with snacks piled high,
We share silly stories, oh me, oh my!
A squirrel in a hat acts quite the fool,
We laugh till we snort, it's the best kind of school.

With marshmallows toasted, we craft our own dreams,
Imagining worlds where nothing's as it seems.
A raccoon in slippers plays cards with a crow,
And giggles erupt, as we all steal the show.

The stars seem to wink, as if in on the joke,
While an elf drops his candy, oh what a poke!
We're dancing with shadows, we twirl and we spin,
In whimsical nights, let the fun now begin!

So raise up a glass, to memories we make,
Every chuckle and giggle is now ours to stake.
In cherished moments, we let our hearts soar,
With whimsical nights, who could ask for more?

The Magic of Kindred Spirits

In the glow of friendship, we find our true selves,
Like mismatched socks sitting on dusty shelves.
With quirky adventures that sprinkle our days,
We're weird and we're wild, in so many ways.

We plot out our schemes like a band of old pros,
Taking awkward steps in our flip-flop shoes,
A walrus on wheels makes a splash with a grin,
In this magic of kinship, we always win!

So share in the laughter, the secrets, the plans,
We take on the world with butter and cans!
In silly embraces, we find our own art,
With kindred spirits, we each play our part.

As we clink our hot drinks, let's toast to the fun,
For magic is real when we're all on the run.
Dear friends, let's be silly, let's dance 'till we fall,
In the magic of spirits, we're having a ball!

Cocoa Clouds and Cozy Snuggles

Hot cocoa is steaming, with marshmallows afloat,
We pile on the blankets, this is our boat.
Gazing out the window, oh what a surprise,
A penguin in pajamas is flapping his thighs!

With stories of bears who wear funky hats,
We giggle at tales of well-mannered cats.
A foot race to the fridge for a cookie or two,
We sprinkle the night with giggles and goo.

In cocoa clouds, we drift off to dream,
Of dancing on rainbows and climbing a beam.
A cozy cocoon that we cherish like gold,
With snuggles and laughter, our hearts we unfold.

So let's savor these moments, let's hold them real tight,
In cocoa clouds and cozy, warm, snuggly nights.
For laughter is sweeter than any delight,
Together, dear friends, we'll shine ever bright!

A Canvas of Laughter and Love

In a world where giggles reign,
Painted smiles wipe away the pain.
With crayons bright and laughter loud,
We color life, so joyful, so proud.

From tickles, jokes, a playful shove,
Our hearts are full, a canvas of love.
We draw the quirks of our weird crew,
With every smile, we make art too.

Each splatter of fun, a masterpiece,
In quirky hues, our worries cease.
So come with me, let's dance and play,
Creating laughs, come what may!

Laughter's brush, in each odd hue,
A joyful scene, just me and you.
So take a seat, enjoy the show,
This canvas grows, and faces glow!

Chimes of Blessings in the Air

With each chime, a blessing rings,
Like Santa's sleigh that laughter brings.
Bells jingle joy, as pie falls flat,
Oops! Who forgot the welcome mat?

In this symphony, we dance and sway,
Each stumble adds to our ballet.
Giggling softly at our plight,
At least we shine with all our might!

The heavens chuckle, a playful wink,
As we try to pour without a drink.
Happiness echoes loud and clear,
Who knew blessings tasted like beer?

So here's to the moments, the chimes that play,
Laughter's melody brightens our day.
Together we share, both joy and cheer,
In each ringing laugh, our love is near!

The Warmth of Togetherness

In a blanket fort, we huddle tight,
Sharing stories 'til the fall of night.
With marshmallow dreams and cocoa smiles,
Laughter will linger for a while.

Each silly face and goofy dance,
In this warm space, we find our chance.
To drop all worries, let our guard down,
Wearing our giggles like a crown.

Hilarity wraps us in cozy glow,
Even when the fence is low.
With every chuckle, we build a nest,
In this hum of laughter, we feel our zest.

So let us gather, and love what's true,
With goofy grins, just me and you.
In this warmth, we bravely share
The simple joy of being there!

Floating Wishes on Frosty Breezes

On frosty mornings, we slip and slide,
Chasing wishes down winter's ride.
Snowflakes twirl, like dreams in flight,
Who needs a hat? It's all pure delight!

With snickers and giggles, our breath puffs out,
Creating clouds with every shout.
Sledding adventures, fun at its peak,
Laughter erupts; we play hide and seek.

The frost nips lightly at our red noses,
While snowmen laugh at our winter poses.
With each cold snap that makes us freeze,
We warm our hearts, as we tease with ease.

So let the chilly winds freely blow,
Together we stand, in laughter's glow.
On frosty wishes, our joy does ride,
In this winter wonderland, side by side!

Hearts Entwined in Festive Play

Two hearts collide like snowballs round,
Laughter erupts with a silly sound.
As we trip over tinsel and cheer,
The dog steals the turkey, oh dear!

Gingerbread men run for their lives,
They know our baking skills—where's the prize?
We dance 'round the tree with great delight,
In our mismatched socks, we'll outshine the night.

Hot cocoa spills while we giggle and snack,
With marshmallows flying, it's a wild attack.
We'll toast to the chaos, our hearts in a whirl,
In this festive mess, we'll give it a twirl.

So raise up your cups, let merriment flow,
We'll laugh at our blunders and let nothing slow.
For hearts entwined in this jolly dismay,
Will forever remember this festive play!

Shimmering Eyes and Soft Goodbyes

Shimmering eyes, a sight so sweet,
As we swap gifts, oh what a treat!
A tie for Dad, a book for the kid,
A cactus for Mom—who knows what I did?

With cookies and laughs, we circle the room,
Then suddenly pause—uh-oh, there's doom!
My aunt sings a song that lasts for an hour,
While we all sit frozen, with dwindling power.

Soft goodbyes drift like snowflakes from lips,
With hugs so tight, not one slip of grip.
We'll remember this night for the joy and the fun,
But mostly the chaos from everyone!

So raise your glass to every bright cheer,
And thank all the mishaps that brought us near.
With shimmering eyes and joy in the skies,
We'll treasure these moments, not saying goodbyes!

A Palette of Festive Emotions

A palette bright with colors so bold,
Red for the laughter, green for the cold.
Blue for the baking disasters galore,
And yellow for joy bursting out from each door.

Each brushstroke tells tales of mishaps sincere,
Like Aunt Judy's hat that's awfully near.
With sprinkles of chaos in shades of delight,
Our festive emotions are quite the sight!

The canvas of cheer stretches wide and far,
As family gatherings raise the bizarre.
Pink for the blush from that awkward song,
And orange for all of us singing along.

So dip into this art, let it brighten your day,
With laughter and love, come what may.
A palette of moments we cherish, no doubt,
In this festive playground, together we shout!

The Spirit of Giving Blooms

The spirit of giving blooms like a flower,
With gifts wrapped in paper, we gather the power.
To spread joy and laughter, oh what a thrill,
As we dodge Grandma's secret recipe skills!

We unwrap the surprises, some silly and sweet,
A pair of socks and a toy for our feet.
We giggle at gifts, the trials and the plight,
Like my cousin's old sweater, a truly bad sight!

The joy of the season is more than just stuff,
It's sharing a snack or a moment of fluff.
With cookies and hugs, and stories we swap,
The spirit of giving just won't ever stop!

So let's raise a cheer, and take a good look,
At the laughter we share in this holiday book.
With every small gesture, let the love loom,
For the spirit of giving is sure to bloom!

Gleeful Feet on Winter Streets

Snowflakes swirl, a blissful dance,
Children giggle, take a chance.
Slipping, sliding, on their way,
Winter's joy, come out to play.

Hot cocoa spills, oh what a sight,
Marshmallows drift, oh what a flight.
Laughter echoes, as they fall,
Gleeful feet, we hear their call.

Frosty noses, cheeks so red,
Chasing snowballs, oh, in dread.
Tumbles and giggles fill the air,
Winter fun is everywhere!

Homeward bound with cheeks aglow,
Next time, careful, take it slow.
Memories made with each snowball,
Gleeful hearts, we loved it all!

Spices and Sweets of Remembrance

Baking cookies, oh what a smell,
Cinnamon whispers, all is well.
Gingerbread men, they dance and sway,
Frosted treats brighten our day.

Nutmeg dreams and pecan pies,
Sugar sprinkles like starry skies.
Lemon zests and chocolate bliss,
Each sweet treat holds a little kiss.

Grandma's stories, love we recall,
Every bite, a memory's call.
Laughter rings 'round cookie sheets,
Spices stir up joyful feats.

With every nibble, joy expands,
Sweets and spices in our hands.
Oh what bliss, our hearts do sing,
In every bite, the joy they bring!

A Symphony of Joyful Echoes

Laughter bounces off the walls,
In joyful echoes, fun enthralls.
Tickles, giggles, silly sounds,
In this symphony, joy abounds.

A trumpet blasts from someone's nose,
A chorus of "what's that?" explodes.
Puppies join in with little barks,
Creating music at the parks.

Dancing feet make the rhythm sway,
In a playful, merry ballet.
With friends all gathered, hearts so bright,
A symphony of pure delight.

As sunset paints the sky with gold,
This orchestra of laughter bold.
Let the echoes drift and play,
In joyful harmony, we stay!

Beneath the Mistletoe's Warm Glow

Underneath the berry bow,
A timid glance, oh, don't be slow.
Kisses stolen, cheeks a-flame,
Mistletoe's magic plays its game.

Awkward shuffles, giggles shared,
Nervous smiles, the moment bared.
With every peck, the laughter grows,
Beneath the mistletoe's warm glow.

Uncle Joe thinks it's a treat,
Winks and nudges, can't feel his feet.
A holiday blush, a festive thrill,
Love's sweet bloom gives hearts a chill.

It's truly grand this time of year,
Full of joy, warmth, and cheer.
So gather 'round, the love will flow,
Beneath the mistletoe's warm glow!

Frost-kissed Wishes in the Night Air

Snowflakes dance, a silly sight,
They land on noses, a soft delight.
Whispers swirled in winter's cheer,
Hot cocoa spills, oh dear, oh dear!

Frosty breath in the chilly breeze,
As penguins stroll with utmost ease.
The moon winks down, it's quite absurd,
I swear it just chuckled, how absurd!

Candles flicker, shadows fight,
With marshmallow fluff in every bite.
Snowmen grinning in hats cocked,
Who knew winter could be so knocked!

Dreams take flight on frosty nights,
Where laughter hides and joy ignites.
Sleds careen on icy trails,
While hot wings distract from epic fails!

Moments Wrapped in Warmth and Wonder

A cozy nook, my favorite chair,
Wrapped in blankets without a care.
Coffee brews with chocolate swirls,
I spill it all, oh fate unfurls!

Friends arrive with silly snacks,
Chips fly high, laughter attacks.
Conversations buzz like bees,
As cupcakes vanish with such ease!

Socks mismatched, just how I roll,
Chasing after that last meatball.
Games get wild, the chaos reigns,
Who knew joy could burst our veins?

With every bite and every laugh,
We toast to life, the perfect craft.
Moments wrap like s'mores in fire,
A recipe for pure desire!

Illuminated Souls Beneath Starlit Skies

Stars twinkle above, a dazzling show,
While we sing off-key, putting on a glow.
Campfires crackle with popcorn bursts,
Somebody's jacket? Oh, whoops, it's yours!

The night was cool, yet hearts were warm,
With ghost stories that twist and swarm.
Marshmallows toasted to golden perfection,
The sugar rush causes wild connection!

Fireflies wink in sly disguise,
As we dance with laughter, under moonlit skies.
Falling over, then bursting in cheer,
Who knew stumbles could be so dear?

Together we shine like the stars so bright,
In our heartbeats, we find delight.
Moments caught beneath that dome,
Illuminated, we're truly home!

Laughter in the Air, Love Everywhere

In parks where puppies prance around,
Laughter echoes, a joyful sound.
With frisbees flying and snacks that lag,
You topple over – oh, what a brag!

Picnic baskets full of cheer,
Silly hats and summer beer.
Friends with jokes that dance and twirl,
Spills and giggles, a pocket swirl!

Squirrels dart and snatch a fry,
With sneaky moves, oh my, oh my!
As laughter ricochets off trees,
Love blooms quietly, with such ease.

Under the sun, life's perfect treat,
With every hug, our hearts repeat.
Through hiccups, spills, and joyful glare,
Laughter floats, love fills the air!

The Magic of Togetherness Unfolds

In a kitchen filled with chatter,
Grandma's cookies rise and splatter.
Cousins dance in socks so bright,
Tumbling over, what a sight!

We're a crew of mismatched socks,
Sneaking snacks and silly talks.
Laughter echoes, time does fly,
Together, we can almost fly!

Board games turn into great feuds,
As we tease our rival broods.
Who knew family could surprise,
With tasty tricks and daring lies?

As night falls, we share our tales,
Of epic highs and silly fails.
With love, we conquer every fold,
The magic of togetherness unfolds!

Radiant Hearts on Frosty Days

Snowflakes swirl like tiny dancers,
As hot cocoa warms our chancers.
Scarves wrapped tight and mittens snug,
Let's build a snowman, give it a hug!

Out we go, it's slippery fun,
Chasing friends just like they run.
Face-plants, giggles, laughter's roar,
In frosty air, we all want more!

Frosty noses, icicles too,
Warming hearts, we know what to do.
Hot chocolate shared with a dash of glee,
Radiant hearts, wild and free!

As the sun sets, our cheeks all glow,
Memories made in a winter show.
With every giggle, every play,
We shine like stars on frosty days!

Gifts of Love in Every Gesture

A simple note tucked near your sock,
Brings a smile like a ticking clock.
A pat on the back, a wink or two,
Gifts of love from me to you.

A cup of tea when the day feels long,
A silly dance, a silly song.
Friendship bracelets made with flair,
Each knot tied with a special care.

A handful of hugs, or just a glance,
Can turn a dull day into a dance.
Filling hearts with joy and laughter,
Gifts of love we're always after!

So share a smile, keep spirits high,
In every gesture, let kindness fly.
Cherished moments, bright and true,
Are the sweetest gifts between me and you!

Unity Found in Twinkling Moments

Under stars, we share our dreams,
With laughter flowing like sweet streams.
Holding hands, we take our stance,
In twinkling moments, we find our dance.

A sparkler fizzles, lights up the night,
While friends giggle with sheer delight.
A chorus of voices, a musical cheer,
Unity found, wrapped up in here.

Inside jokes and silly puns,
Connecting us like shining suns.
In these moments, fears disappear,
With a wink, a smile, and plenty of cheer!

So let's treasure each laugh, each shout,
In this unity, there's no doubt.
As the world spins, we stand like glue,
In twinkling moments, it's me and you!

Candlelight Dreams of Peace and Cheer

In a room filled with candles, oh what a sight,
Dreams of peace dance in the flickering light.
But watch out for shadows, they might steal your chair,
And leave you sitting awkwardly, gasping for air.

With laughter and giggles, we raise our glass high,
To toast to the moments that make us all spry.
Between puffs of the smoke, a joke drifts on by,
Why did the candle feel blue? Oh my!

It couldn't find a match, isn't that sad?
But cheer up, dear candle, don't feel so bad!
For even in darkness, you're bright and you glow,
Just watch for the wind, or your dance gets too slow.

So let's light up the night, share joy, not a frown,
With candlelight dreams, let's twirl all around.
We'll laugh 'til we snort, then we'll giggle some more,
In this glowing adventure, who could ask for more?

Melodies of Hope on a Snowy Eve

Snowflakes are falling, the world's dressed in white,
We gather 'round cozy, it feels just right.
The melodies play as we dance on the floor,
To the jolly old tunes that we hum and adore.

The snowman outside has a carrot for a nose,
But he's lost his top hat, poor fellow! Who knows?
As we sing songs of hope, heartwarming and bright,
That snowman will surely join in our delight!

With mugs filled with cocoa, marshmallows afloat,
We'll sip while we giggle, perhaps spill a boat.
A snowball fight breaks, we unleash all our glee,
And hope that the neighbors don't complain loudly.

So let's wrap this night in laughter and cheer,
With melodies of hope, there's nothing to fear.
On this snowy eve, we'll let our hearts sing,
For love is the song that the season will bring!

Kindness Wrapped in Ribbons and Bows

In boxes of joy, kindness tied up neat,
With ribbons and bows, it's a marvelous treat.
But careful where you step, there's tape on the floor,
You might slip and slide through the kind fest we score!

We'll sprinkle our smiles like glitter in air,
And share all our goodies, that's truly fair.
Just save a few cookies, for my cookie dough,
Or else I might show up in your chimney, oh no!

With hugs and good wishes, we're all feeling grand,
While trying to juggle this tinsel so bland.
"Who wrapped this?" I ask, "With tape strong as glue?"
It's clear that the kitten has been quite the crew!

So kindness wrapped up is our gift for today,
With laughter and joy leading the way.
Let's share what we've got, spread love with each bow,
For kindness will bloom, and it's free, just so you know!

Celebrations Under a Blanket of Snow

Under blankets of snow, let the celebrations start,
With hot drinks and laughter, we open our heart.
We dance in the snow, our feet all a-flop,
But watch for the puddles, or you might just plop!

The tree's brightly lit, shining jewels everywhere,
The ornaments giggle, perfection's laid bare.
We toast to the moments with friends gathered near,
But let's not spill cider—oh dear, oh dear!

With snowflakes like confetti, we shout out a cheer,
As fireworks sparkle, everyone's near.
We build frosty figures, creations so proud,
But one fell apart, and we laughed oh so loud!

So here's to the nights where joy never ceases,
Under blankets of snow, our laughter increases.
Let's dance 'round the tree, and let spirits flow,
In the warmth of our hearts, we'll let our love grow!

Cradled in Joy

Bouncing on clouds, what a sight,
Giggles and laughter dance in the light.
A tickle from joy, it's contagious,
Dancing with glee, oh, it's outrageous!

Like jellybeans spilled on the floor,
Wobbling and wobbling, can't take it anymore.
With each silly face, our spirits grow,
Cradled in joy, just go with the flow.

Frogs in tuxedos croak a sweet tune,
As squirrels in top hats join in the boon.
Together we sing, without any care,
Cradled in joy, with laughter to share.

So bring out the cupcakes, let's eat and play,
In this strange land where silliness stays.
With friends by our side, what more could we want?
Cradled in joy, let's party and flaunt!

Hearts Unite

In a world of mismatched socks,
We gather like playful frocks.
Hearts unite, oh what a cheer,
A big hug shared, never fear!

Like jelly on toast, we spread our glee,
Together we laugh, wild and free.
Hearts unite with a wild dance,
A silly jig, oh, give it a chance!

Like cookies that crumble with sweet delight,
We stick together, what a glorious sight!
In the chaos, we find our groove,
With hearts in sync, we can't help but move!

So here's to the quirks that make us whole,
With laughter and love, we reach our goal.
In this silly world, take my hand,
For hearts unite, together we stand!

Sugarplum Wishes in the Moonlight

Under the stars, we twirl and sway,
Sugarplum wishes dance in the fray.
Whispers of sweetness fill the air,
As moonbeams tease without a care.

Like fairies on cupcakes, we flitter about,
With sprinkles of laughter, we twist and shout.
Each wish is a giggle, each star a delight,
In the soft glow of fun, we take flight.

Mice with top hats join in the fun,
Sipping sweet dreams until they are done.
With candy canes swinging and friends side by side,
Sugarplum wishes we'll never hide!

So here's to the magic that shines from above,
In moonlight, together, we find our love.
With wishes like balloons, we rise and play,
Under the night sky, let's dance till the day!

Hues of Joy in the Winter's Glow

Snowflakes spin in a dance so grand,
Hues of joy sprinkle across the land.
We build a snowman, round and tall,
With a carrot hat, he'll never fall!

Hot cocoa warms our chilly hands,
Marshmallows bounce like fluffy bands.
Laughter echoes as snowballs fly,
In hues of joy, we reach for the sky.

With playful penguins leading the way,
Join us in this whimsical play.
Sledding down hills, we laugh with glee,
In winter's glow, come share with me!

So gather your friends, let's shine so bright,
In this playful world, everything's right.
With hues of joy wrapped in snow's embrace,
Let's celebrate winter with smiles on our face!

A Symphony of Smiles and Sweet Treats

In the kitchen, we mix and we stir,
Creating a chaos that's sure to concur.
With sprinkles and frosting, oh what a sight,
A symphony of smiles, pure delight!

Chocolate chips hop in with a cheer,
As laughter echoes, bringing us near.
Cookies on trays, all golden and round,
Sweet treats united, joy is found!

The oven is humming a merry tune,
While sugar dreams float like a balloon.
Together we bake, the fun never ends,
In this sweet journey, we're all best friends!

So grab a cupcake, take a big bite,
A symphony of sweetness, everything's right.
With smiles and laughter, we build our fleet,
So here's to the joy of our sweetened retreat!

Milton Keynes UK
Ingram Content Group UK Ltd.
UKHW021403081224
452111UK00007B/126